FULL-COLOR SOURCEBOOK OF
FRENCH
FASHION
15ᵀᴴ TO 19ᵀᴴ CENTURIES

DRAWN AND ENGRAVED BY

PAUQUET FRÈRES

DOVER PUBLICATIONS, INC.
MINEOLA, NEW YORK

Bibliographical Note

This Dover edition, first published in 2003, is a selection of 76 plates from the original collection of 96 that comprises *Modes et Costumes Historiques* from the *Bureaux des Modes et Costumes Historiques*. The work was originally published c. 1864 by René Pincebourde, Paris, and it is very scarce, even among specialists in rare books.

DOVER *Pictorial Archive* SERIES

Library of Congress Cataloging-in-Publication Data

Modes et costumes historiques. Selections.
    Full-color sourcebook of French fashion : 15th to 19th centuries / drawn and engraved by Pauquet frères.
        p. cm. — (Dover pictorial archive series)
    In French.
    A selection of 76 plates from the original collection of 96 drawn by Hippolyte Louis Emile Pauquet and Polydore Jean Charles Pauquet published: Pauquet frères : R. Pincebourde, [18—].
    ISBN 0-486-42838-9 (pbk.)
    1. Costume—France—History—Pictorial works. I. Pauquet, Hippolyte Louis Emile, b. 1797. II. Pauquet, Polydore Jean Charles, b. 1800. III. Pauquet frères (Firm) IV. Title. V. Series.
GT853.M632 2003
391'.00944'0222—dc21

                                                                            2003043451

Manufactured in the United States of America
Dover Publications, Inc., 31 East 2nd Street, Mineola, N.Y. 11501

LIST OF PLATES

FIFTEENTH CENTURY

1. Princess (reign of Charles VI), 1420
2. Eude-Juvénal des Ursins (reign of Charles VI), 1420
3. Women from the outskirts of Paris (reign of Charles VII), 1443
4. Paris Fashion (reign of Charles VII), 1450
5. Chambermaid (reign of Charles VII), 1460
6. Lady of Quality (reign of Charles VII), 1460
7. Shepherdess (reign of Charles VIII), 1491
8. Courtesan (reign of Charles VIII), 1491
9. Baron and Baroness (reign of Charles VIII), 1493
10. Doctor (reign of Charles VIII), 1493

SIXTEENTH CENTURY

11. Page (reign of Louis XII), 1500
12. Anne de Bretagne (2nd wife of Louis XII), 1500
13. Burgher (reign of Louis XII), 1510
14. Henri d'Albret (grandfather of Henri IV), 1527
15. Eléonore d'Autriche (2nd wife of François I), 1530
16. François (eldest son of François I), 1534
17. Gentleman (reign of Charles IX), 1572
18. Lady at Court (reign of Charles IX), 1579
19. Ladies at Court (reign of Henri III), 1580
20. Lady at Court (reign of Henri III), 1580
21. Anne [sic], Duke de Joyeuse (favorite of Henri III), 1581
22. Street-porter (reign of Henri III), 1586
23. Maidservant (reign of Henri III), 1586
24. Gentleman (reign of Henri III), 1586
25. Damsel (reign of Henri III), 1586
26. Henri IV (King of France), 1595

SEVENTEENTH CENTURY

27. Nobility of Lorraine (reign of Louis XIII), 1625
28. Nobility of Lorraine (reign of Louis XIII), 1625
29. French Attire (reign of Louis XIII), 1633
30. Lord (reign of Louis XIII), 1633
31. Town Attire (reign of Louis XIII), 1633
32. Gentleman (reign of Louis XIII), 1642
33. Mlle de la Vallière (reign of Louis XIV), 1661
34. Prince (reign of Louis XIV), 1670
35. Milkmaid with Headdress (reign of Louis XIV), 1680
36. Lady of Quality (reign of Louis XIV), 1692
37. Duchess of Orléans (reign of Louis XIV), 1692
38. Fashionably-attired Knight (reign of Louis XIV), 1693
39. Duchess (reign of Louis XIV), 1693
40. Lady of Quality in a Dressing Gown (reign of Louis XIV), 1696

PLATE 1. Princess (reign of Charles VI), 1420

PLATE 2. Eude-Juvénal des Ursins (reign of Charles VI), 1420

PLATE 3. Women from the outskirts of Paris (reign of Charles VII), 1443

PLATE 4. Paris Fashion (reign of Charles VII), 1450

PLATE 5. Chambermaid (reign of Charles VII), 1460

PLATE 6. Lady of Quality (reign of Charles VII), 1460

PLATE 7. Shepherdess (reign of Charles VIII), 1491

PLATE 8. Courtesan (reign of Charles VIII), 1491

PLATE 9. Baron and Baroness (reign of Charles VIII), 1493

PLATE 10. Doctor (reign of Charles VIII), 1493

PLATE 11. Page (reign of Louis XII), 1500

PLATE 12. Anne de Bretagne (2nd wife of Louis XII), 1500

PLATE 13. Burgher (reign of Louis XII), 1510

PLATE 14. Henri d'Albret (grandfather of Henri IV), 1527

PLATE 15. Eléonore d'Autriche (2nd wife of François I), 1530

PLATE 16. François (eldest son of François I), 1534

PLATE 17. Gentleman (reign of Charles IX), 1572

PLATE 18. Lady at Court (reign of Charles IX), 1579

PLATE 19. Ladies at Court (reign of Henri III), 1580

PLATE 20. Lady at Court (reign of Henri III), 1580

PLATE 21. Anne [*sic*], Duke de Joyeuse (favorite of Henri III), 1581

PLATE 22. Street-porter (reign of Henri III), 1586

PLATE 23. Maidservant (reign of Henri III), 1586

PLATE 24. Gentleman (reign of Henri III), 1586

PLATE 25. Damsel (reign of Henri III), 1586

PLATE 26. Henri IV (King of France), 1595

PLATE 27. Nobility of Lorraine (reign of Louis XIII), 1625

PLATE 28. Nobility of Lorraine (reign of Louis XIII), 1625

PLATE 29. French Attire (reign of Louis XIII), 1633

PLATE 30. Lord (reign of Louis XIII), 1633

PLATE 31. Town Attire (reign of Louis XIII), 1633

PLATE 32. Gentleman (reign of Louis XIII), 1642

PLATE 33. Mlle de la Vallière (reign of Louis XIV), 1661

PLATE 34. Prince (reign of Louis XIV), 1670

PLATE 35. Milkmaid with Headdress (reign of Louis XIV), 1680

PLATE 36. Lady of Quality (reign of Louis XIV), 1692

PLATE 37. Duchess of Orléans (reign of Louis XIV), 1692

PLATE 38. Fashionably-attired Knight (reign of Louis XIV), 1693

PLATE 39. Duchess (reign of Louis XIV), 1693

PLATE 40. Lady of Quality in a Dressing Gown (reign of Louis XIV), 1696

PLATE 41. Fashionably–attired Knight (reign of Louis XIV), 1700

PLATE 42. Fashionably-attired Knight (reign of Louis XIV), 1706

PLATE 43. Dresses with Hoop Petticoats (reign of Louis XV), 1729

PLATE 44. Mlle Sallé (reign of Louis XV), 1730

PLATE 45. Marchioness (reign of Louis XV), 1740

PLATE 46. Paris Fashion, Lady of the Nobility (reign de Louis XV), 1740

PLATE 47. Marquis (reign of Louis XV), 1740

PLATE 48. Paris Fashion (reign of Louis XV), 1740

PLATE 49. Court Attire (reign of Louis XV), 1745

PLATE 50. Mme Pompadour (reign of Louis XV), 1746

PLATE 51. Paris Fashion (reign of Louis XV), 1763

PLATE 52. Mme du Barry (reign of Louis XV), 1770

PLATE 53. Paris Fashion (reign of Louis XVI), 1777

PLATE 54. Paris Fashion (reign of Louis XVI), 1777

PLATE 55. Duchess (reign of Louis XVI), 1783

PLATE 56. Paris Fashion (reign of Louis XVI), 1787

PLATE 57. Marie-Antoinette (Queen of France), 1788

PLATE 58. Paris Fashion (reign of Louis XVI), 1790

PLATE 59. Paris Fashion (reign of Louis XVI—Revolution), 1792

PLATE 60. Paris Fashion (reign of Louis XVI—Revolution), 1792

PLATE 61. Paris Fashion (reign of Louis XVI—Revolution), 1792

PLATE 62. Paris Fashion (French Republic—Revolution), 1793

PLATE 63. Paris Fashion (National Convention), 1795

PLATE 64. Paris Fashion (National Convention), 1795

PLATE 65. "The Folly of the Day" (Directory), 1798

PLATE 66. A Duellist (Directory), 1798

PLATE 67. Paris Fashion (Directory), 1798

PLATE 68. Attire for a Fancy Dress Ball (Consulate), 1801

PLATE 69. Town Attire (Consulate), 1803

PLATE 70. Informal Attire (Empire), 1807

PLATE 71. Ladies of Paris (Empire), 1813

PLATE 72. Court Attire (reign of Louis XVIII), 1816

PLATE 73. Attire for a Fancy Dress Ball (reign of Louis XVIII), 1819

PLATE 74. Paris Fashion (reign of Louis XVIII), 1820

PLATE 75. Paris Fashion (reign of Charles X), 1828

PLATE 76. Ladies of Paris (Empire [Napoleon III]), 1864